AUTHOR
AND
FINISHER

Unleash the Power of Faith: Embrace Jesus, the Author and Finisher

ELIZABETH OLUFEMI

Author and Finisher

Copyright © 2023 Elizabeth Olufemi

All rights reserved. No part of this book may be reproduced or trans mitted in any form or by any means without the written permission of the author.

Scriptures marked KJV are taken from the KING JAMES VERSION (KJV): KING JAMES VERSION, public domain.

Scripture taken from the New King James Version®. Copyright © 1982 by Thomas Nelson. Used by permission. All rights reserved. Scripture quotations marked (NIV) are taken from the Holy Bible, New International Version®, NIV®. Copyright © 1973, 1978, 1984, 2011 by Biblica, Inc.™ Used by permission of Zondervan.

All rights reserved worldwide. www.zondervan.com. The "NIV" and "New International Version" are trademarks registered in the United States Patent and Trademark Office by Biblica, Inc.™.

Scriptures marked AMP are taken from the AMPLIFIED BIBLE (AMP): Scripture taken from the AMPLIFIED® BIBLE, Copyright © 1954, 1958, 1962, 1964, 1965, 1987 by the Lockman Foundation Used by Permission. (www.Lockman.org)

Published by:
Eleviv Publishing Group
Centerville, OH 45458
info@elevivpublishing.com
www.elevivpublishing.com

ISBN: (PB) 978-1-952744-80-8
         (E-book) 978-1-952744-81-5

Printed in the United States of America

FOREWARD

It is with great pleasure and anticipation that I write the foreword for *"Author and Finisher."* This book is a powerful exploration of the central role Jesus plays in our faith journey, reminding us that He is not only the Author but also the Finisher of our lives.

In a world filled with uncertainty and constant change, it is essential to anchor our faith in something unshakeable. And who better to entrust our lives to than Jesus Christ? As the Author of all creation, He intricately weaves together the story of our existence, infusing it with purpose, meaning, and divine guidance.

"Author and Finisher" invites readers on a transformative journey, one that will challenge, inspire, and deepen their understanding of the depth of God's love. Through personal anecdotes, biblical insights, and a keen understanding of the human experience, the author guides us toward a greater appreciation for the role Jesus plays in our lives.

From the moment we surrender our lives to Christ, He takes the pen in His hand, ready to script a beautiful and awe-inspiring story. But this journey is not without its challenges. We face trials, doubts, and setbacks along the way. Yet, in those moments, we discover the unwavering faithfulness of Jesus, who is not only the Author but also the Finisher of our faith. He never abandons us in the midst of the storm but leads us through it, refining us and molding us into His image.

"Author and Finisher" is a timely reminder of the eternal truth that Jesus is the centerpiece of our faith. Through captivating storytelling, sound biblical teaching, and heartfelt personal reflections, the author encourages readers to fix their eyes on Jesus, to press on through adversity, and to continually seek His guidance.

As you embark on this journey within the pages of *"Author and Finisher,"* I encourage you to open your heart and mind to the transformative power of Jesus' love. Allow Him to write a new chapter in your life, to guide your steps, and to bring you into a deeper relationship with Him. May this book inspire and equip you to live a life of purpose, impact, and unwavering faith.

In the end, as you close this book, may you be filled with a renewed sense of hope and a burning desire to walk alongside the Author and Finisher of your faith, trusting that He is faithful to bring your story to its glorious conclusion.

Blessings on your journey,
Vivian Elebiyo-Okojie

DEDICATION

This book is dedicated to the author and finisher of my faith, King Jesus. Your grace and favor has been my shield for such a time as this.

ACKNOWLEDGMENT

To my sweet and amazing mother, Juliana Olufemi for staying beside me during those dark moments and ensuring that I got the best care possible. Thank you so much for your sacrifices. A true mother you are!

To my best friend and motivator Mr. Diamond, thank you so much for your unwavering support when I needed suggestions or making a selection. I am so grateful.

To my princes and princess, Joseph, Isaiah, and Isabelle for your support and understanding when mommy needed to put in some work. I am so blessed and I love you all.

A special thanks to Vivian Okojie, *CEO of Eleviv Publishing* who was recommended by the woman of God Queen Belema Abili. To the entire team for bringing my story to life, and for all your support.

To my amazing siblings Samuel and Yemisi Olufemi for you unwavering love and support. Thank you sis for offering suggestions towards this book.

Special thanks to my friend and spiritual mentor Prophet James for all your prayers and encouragement during the ups and downs. I pray for more anointing.

To my amazing brethren in Christ, thank you for taking the time to read my book. God bless!

TABLE OF CONTENT

Introduction
The Architect of Our Faith

1. The Foundation ... *10*
Understanding the Role of Jesus as Author and Finisher

2. The Companion ... *27*
The Role of the Holy Spirit in Our Faith Journey

3. Embracing the Worst-Case Scenario ... *33*
The Power of Scripture and Faith in Adversity

4. Faith as a Guiding Force ... *40*
Finding Purpose in the Midst of Struggle

5. Cultivating a Heart of Gratitude ... *45*

6. The Ongoing Project ... *51*
Growing in Faith through Life's Challenges

7. Spiritual Disciplines ... *57*
Tools for Building a Stronger Faith

8. Jesus as the Finisher ... *62*
The Promise of Eternal Life

9. The Masterpiece ... *67*
Living a Life of Purpose and Impact

10. A Never-Ending Story ... *70*
Continuing Our Journey with Jesus

11. The Author's Return ... *73*
Anticipating the Second Coming of Christ

Conclusion
Embracing the Author and Finisher of Our Faith

INTRODUCTION
The Architect of Our Faith

In the ever-changing landscape of our lives, finding a stable foundation upon which to build our faith can be challenging. As we embark on our spiritual journey, we may find ourselves navigating various beliefs, practices, and teachings.

Amidst this complexity, we often seek a guiding force to help us make sense of our experiences and lead us toward a deeper, more meaningful relationship with the Divine. *"Author and Finisher"* is a book dedicated to exploring the central role of Jesus Christ in our spiritual journey as the architect of our faith.

Throughout history, Jesus has been recognized as the cornerstone of Christian belief. As fully human and divine, He bridges humanity and God, inviting us into a transformative relationship with the Creator. In this book, we will delve into the concept of Jesus as the Author and Finisher of our faith, examining how He initiates, nurtures, and completes our spiritual journey. I will also share some of my personal spiritual journey and stories with you.

Drawing from Scripture, Christian theology, and the experiences of believers throughout the ages, we will journey together through the life and teachings of Jesus Christ, exploring His role as the foundation of our faith. We will investigate the significance of His life, death, and resurrection and the implications these events have for our spiritual development. By examining the various facets of our relationship with Jesus, we will understand how He supports and guides us in our quest for spiritual growth and fulfillment.

We will explore the practical aspects of deepening our faith, including the Holy Spirit's role, the Christian community's importance, and the value of spiritual disciplines. As we delve into these topics, we will learn how Jesus not only serves as the foundation of our faith but also as the ultimate goal, guiding us toward the promise of eternal life and a glorious reunion with God.

I hope that *"Author and Finisher"* will inspire and equip you with the knowledge and tools necessary to cultivate a vibrant and thriving faith anchored in the life and teachings of Jesus Christ. Whether you are just beginning your spiritual journey or have been walking with Jesus for many years, this book is an invitation to embrace the all-encompassing love of the one who is both the Author and Finisher of our faith. Let us embark on this journey together, trusting in the steadfast guidance of Jesus Christ, the architect of our faith.

1

THE FOUNDATION
Understanding the Role of Jesus as Author and Finisher

Birthday Tragedy

The story of my childhood started when I could vividly remember at the age of five. In 1986, my parents decided to travel back to Nigeria with my three siblings and me. My dad chose not to become a permanent resident in the United States after completing his first and second degrees. It was a tough decision for my mom to accept, but her husband's decision was final.

We packed our bags and left for our home country Nigeria. According to my dad, it was a calling from God for him to fulfill and accomplish his purpose and prophetic calling on his life. We arrived in Lagos, and one could feel the change in atmosphere and new environment compared to where we came from. As we settled in the hotel, our families came visiting with excitement to see us return home.

However, our stay in Lagos was short-lived as we traveled to Kaduna, northern Nigeria. We settled in

Kaduna and quickly adjusted to the new food and the culture shock. I was registered to attend the Seventh Day Adventist school in the following months of my birthday.

I requested my birthday be celebrated the following year, and my parents accepted. On the twenty-sixth of April, families and friends, including neighbors, were invited to the house, as they knew that we had come back to Nigeria from the States. My birthday was memorable; everyone had fun, and my aunts, uncles, and cousins were all present. This day marked the day that would change the trajectory of my life. At dawn, everyone departed to their destinations.

Early the next day, I was laying on the couch in the living room due to a nightmare, and out of fear, I decided to sleep there. The following incident was unknown to me but was narrated by my mom. But I noticed I was in a different environment when I became conscious. I saw that I was taken to the hospital and could feel pain and burning.

What just happened to me? I could not express myself but was waiting for someone to inform me. A few minutes later, my mom called my name, and I could only nod, and she said sorry. "The nurse approached us and informed us that you should be taken to a different clinic or hospital, that they can't treat you." My mom was on the verge of crying, but immediately we went to a different specialist clinic in Kaduna called Unity Hospital.

Furthermore, when we arrived at the hospital, I was taken care of urgently as it was an emergency. I was admitted immediately and placed on intravenous fluids. At that moment, I could feel inflammation and pain around my mouth and feet. The next day I noticed that my pain became severe in both legs, but I could not move and felt the heaviness. The pain I was experiencing was due to a fire accident while I was unconscious at home.

I later realized that the burning sensation resulted from trying to bring me back to consciousness because I was not responding, and they thought I was dead. Likewise, in trying to wake me up, neighbors around suggested using menthol rub that I was probably cold; they said to use urine so I could drink some that it would assist, but still no changes. Also, they used a spoon to hold my tongue down so I would not gnash my teeth which can cause dental problems or damage my tongue.

In addition, my mom gave me the shocker of my life: when the neighbors were trying to revive me, they placed both feet on the stove to warm me up, and my body temperature was cold. My feet were left on fire for almost half an hour then I screamed back to life due to the fire or heat from the stove. I was still unaware of what was happening until I got to the hospital.

That's why I felt so much inflammation around my feet, thus causing swelling with fluids. The nurse had to cut them open and pour some antibiotics on both feet for them to heal and dry up. On the third day I was discharged from the hospital, I was diagnosed with a seizure that had never occurred before. Also, I was given medication to take home to cure the illness. My mom and dad were happy that I was recuperating gradually as I was wide awake.

Worst Case Scenario

The following week was the most challenging in my healing process. I was unable to talk or do things on my own. I was lifted or carried to the restroom or to take a shower. But God knows his name will be glorified through all this, and my time away from school slowed down my education. However, I was visited at home by my teacher and other students.

As days and weeks passed by, things got worse; my feet got infected. My mom began to treat me with antibiotics, but it did not work. I could not sleep at night due to the pain; it was excruciating. There was no improvement, and as a result of this, we decided to visit the hospital where I was first admitted. We got to the hospital, and the nurses and another doctor that saw my condition stated that both feet were seriously infected and beyond repair. They concluded they would have to amputate both legs from the ankle down.

At this point, my mom and I began to cry profusely and asked if there was any other solution besides amputation. We were on the verge of begging before the owner of the specialist hospital walked in and asked my mom, "Madam, why are you crying"? My mom replied by stating my case and what they were about to do to her baby. The doctor said, "They will not amputate her legs." One time, a church anniversary was celebrated; my parents had to take me to my cousin's place to stay over the weekend to avoid people asking me what was wrong with me.

Also, to add to the smell emanating from the cast on my feet for over a month. After the anniversary party, I was brought back home but had to return to the hospital a week later. One thing I learned during this accident was to be strong and know that tomorrow will be better than yesterday. Every new day that comes brings something new.

The day came for me to go to the hospital to take the cast off. I could remember vividly how my half-brother carried me while my mom followed behind into the theatre. Fear gripped me as I saw all the surgical equipment that was about to be used to remove the cast.

I thought I would probably be given anesthesia or pain medication; unfortunately, it was not the case. I was placed on the surgical bed, and the removal process started. In the removal process, the cast was found to have stuck on my skin like raw meat.

The doctor and nurse had difficulty and were using different solutions to remove the cast stuck, which was the worst experience of my life. With the pain, screaming, and crying, the team removed the cast eventually. There was calmness and expression of success. The wounds were cleaned with a solution and bandage for them to heal. Now the healing process is just beginning. I had soreness and discomfort as I was carried out to be taken home.

In all this, I still believe I will walk again one day. Every few days, I was taken back to the hospital for my wounds to be cleaned to avoid infection. Miraculously, the wound began to heal, and I noticed gradually it started closing. Then one day, I was still on bandages on both feet. I decided to try and stand on my feet because, at that stage, I was tired of using my knees to move around the house.

Also, I just don't want to continue to depend on people around me for help. My mom had a pair of shoes she came to Nigeria with from the States that were very comfy and would not add too much pressure under my fragile feet.

Another thing I noticed was that while my feet were healing, the left foot was not growing that much and was different in size from my left. But that was not something I decided to worry about except to stand and walk one day. There was no therapist to help or assist in moving my feet muscle.

The Miracle Walk

The one who had known me before I was conceived in my mother's womb knows my tomorrow and the future. I believe there is nothing we face as humans; God has given us the power to be victorious and overcome. I used my mom's half-sandal wedge shoe on this faithful day to take that step. I held on to the room's wall and stood firmly on my few; I shouted to call my mom and siblings to see me standing.

My mom shed tears of joy seeing her daughter stand again, but it was short-lived as I began to feel discomfort, and a powerful surge of energy, I would call it, ran through my feet as I stood on them. I rested and tried again; it was still painful because the wounds had yet to heal.

However, my wounds were healing; the doctors were amazed as weeks passed, and finally, the bandages were removed. The excitement was too much to contain as my walk became stronger and less painful. There was praise and a shout of joy in the house as they noticed improvements in my walking ability. God was not done with me yet until his name was glorified.

I have learned not to give up no matter how painful and uncomfortable any situation is. Also, it is essential to note that you must get up again when you fall and not just sit there and watch life pass you by. I found myself helpless and pitiful, but I was tired of crawling on my knee, and seeing other kids playing around was devasting. This I have applied to my life as I grow older, get up again even if you fall. I fell a few times before my walk grew stronger. Every day is a blessing, and knowing God has given us the strong will to face impossible challenges.

During my healing process, God helped me develop my faith, which grew stronger. Even the Bible could prove that *"if our faith is as little as a mustard seed, we can speak to the mountain to move, and it will move" Matt. 17: 20.* Since I was born in a Christian home and my dad was a pastor, knowing God as the Author and Finisher of my faith was imperative.

Also, as Christians, we are not exempted from trials and tribulations. All these help shape and build one's relationship with God. Likewise, one lesson I have learned from this is never to give up even when nothing seems to be improving or happening. One time anxiety crept in, and the thoughts, doubts, and fear invaded my spirit. Even at a young age, I knew to trust God for the impossible.

He is the God of the impossible because he knows the beginning and end. The Author and Finisher knew my beginning; he knew all that would transpire in my journey through life for his name to be glorified.

After that traumatic experience, I was able to go back to school but have missed a great deal of time around a year. However, I was able to catch up with elementary class and with the help of my teacher and classmates. God renewed my strength even when I was weak and overwhelmed with returning to school.

I had to wear socks and comfy shoes because I could still feel the pain and discomfort from the fire accident whenever I stood for too long or walked. Also, my school gave me a little convenience when punishment was awarded to the whole class. That might sound funny, but that is how the system works.

Second Incident

I was not out of the woods yet regarding my health scare. It was a year after the first incident or a convulsion episode like it was called during those times. I was sleeping one morning and had no idea what had happened to me, but I woke up and saw that I was surrounded by my family, who were a little downcast and moody due to what had occurred. I noticed I was in pain inside my mouth. When I asked what happened, I was told that I had an episode of convulsion, and they tried to keep my teeth from biting my tongue, so there was soreness around my gums and tongue. I had to be taken to the hospital to ensure I was alright and see if any medication could stop what was happening.

After the second incident, the doctor prescribed phenobarbital medication to prevent any future occurrence. I started to use this medication and, at the same time, believed that it would work for me. Months passed, even years, and I never experienced such a health scare anymore.

As I mentioned in the previous chapter, it takes us to have faith, even if it is a little like a mustard seed. Even when it does not happen immediately, just believing and trusting God for our request will come to pass if we do not grow weary or give up. Also, a believer in Christ must emulate faith because we cannot please God without it.

The Faith Factor

Every day that passes by brings me closer to what God has destined for me, even while those obstacles or delays are coming to deter my path in life. With my strong will and God's grace, I refuse to give up or let that stop me from accomplishing the purpose of my presence here on earth.

In addition, I beg you not to give up no matter how many afflictions one goes through; it is to make one stronger.

God of grace and mercy will always see one through it all.

Also, I would like to refer that we cannot please God without faith. It is crucial to see the desired results. For example, it is like planting a seed and watching it grow. But to see the flower bud, one needs to water, prune, and even place it outside to receive sunlight. Since I was a pastor's daughter, there were so many expectations from people in the congregation. But one thing that people cannot control is their faith or walk with God.

As I flashback to how I faced those challenges, one thing that always resonates with me is not to give up because tomorrow will be better. Please, I urge you to believe and let your faith levels rise. Sometimes, it can be difficult to believe that things will get better. But as the saying goes, *"With God, all things are possible."* He is the God of the impossible! When I was told my feet would be amputated, I felt my world crashing down at a young age. Deciding to get up took a lot of faith because I might still be wallowing in my pain if I had doubted.

How much faith is required? As little as a mustard seed. That is enough to see you through those challenges or trials if you do not give up. God has instilled in us the willpower to be victorious and overcome obstacles and situations that comes our way. In addition, just know that everything that transpired in one's life is bound to happen simultaneously. It was meant to shape me and build my faith at a young age. Another point about faith is that it is counted as righteousness towards people in the Bible, like Abraham.

Is it not extraordinary to be considered or viewed as a man and woman of faith? There is so much to life; seeing that miracle happens takes only a little effort.

In the hectic pace of modern life, it is easy to lose sight of our existence's true purpose and meaning. As we grapple with the struggles and challenges that come our way, we may find ourselves searching for a stable foundation to build our lives. For many, this foundation is found in Jesus Christ, described in *Hebrews 12:2* as the *"author and finisher of our faith."* In this chapter, we will explore the significance of Jesus as the foundation of our faith, drawing from Scripture and personal anecdotes to gain a deeper understanding of His role in our spiritual journey.

First, let us consider the meaning of the phrase *"author and finisher of our faith."* The word *"author"* can be understood as the initiator or originator of something, while *"finisher"* refers to the one who brings a task to completion. In the context of our faith, Jesus is both the one who initiates our relationship with God and the one who brings it to fruition. This concept is beautifully illustrated in the words of the Apostle Paul in *Philippians 1:6: "Being confident of this very thing, that He who has begun a good work in you will complete it until the day of Jesus Christ."*

To appreciate the significance of Jesus as the Author and Finisher of our faith, we must understand the profound impact of His life, death, and resurrection. As Christians, we believe Jesus was a wise teacher, compassionate healer, and the Son of God who took on human flesh to redeem humanity from sin and death. Jesus paid the price for our sins through His sacrificial death on the cross and reconciled us to God, allowing us to enter into a life-transforming relationship with our Creator.

The Gospel of John beautifully captures the divine nature of Jesus and the significance of His coming to earth: *"In the beginning was the Word, and the Word was with God, and the Word was God...And the Word became flesh and dwelt among us, and we beheld His glory, the glory as of the only begotten of the Father, full of grace and truth"* (John 1:1, 14). This passage reminds us that Jesus is the foundation of our faith and embodiment of God's love and grace, inviting us into a life of transformation and growth.

As the Author of our faith, Jesus initiates our relationship with God through the gift of grace. *Ephesians 2:8-9* teaches us that our salvation is not the result of our own efforts, but rather a gift from God: *"For by grace you have been saved through faith, and that not of yourselves; it is the gift of God, not of works, lest anyone should boast."* This idea is reinforced by Jesus' own words in *John 14:6*, where He declares, *"I am the way, the truth, and the life. No one comes to the Father except through Me."* By placing our faith in Jesus and accepting His gift of grace, we embark on a spiritual growth and transformation journey with Jesus as our guide and foundation.

I remember the moment I first recognized the significance of Jesus as the Author of my faith. I had grown up attending church and learning about God. Still, my faith felt superficial and disconnected from my daily life. It wasn't until I experienced a personal crisis that I truly understood the importance of relying on Jesus as the foundation of my faith.

As I cried out to Him in desperation, I experienced an overwhelming sense of peace and assurance that He was with me and would see me through my difficulties. From that moment on, my faith became deeply rooted in Jesus, and I began to see Him as the Author and sustainer of my spiritual journey. After numerous encounters with

God's divine healing and my faith's perfection, I grew even closer to Him.

As the Finisher of our faith, Jesus initiates our relationship with God and brings it to completion. He is the one who continually guides, strengthens, and refines us as we grow in our faith, ensuring that our spiritual journey ultimately leads us to a deeper understanding of God's love and purpose for our lives.

In *2 Corinthians 3:18*, the Apostle Paul writes, *"But we all, with unveiled face, beholding as in a mirror the glory of the Lord, are being transformed into the same image from glory to glory, just as by the Spirit of the Lord."* This passage highlights the transformative power of Jesus in our lives as He molds us into His image and helps us to reflect His love and grace to the world around us.

One of the most powerful ways Jesus serves as the Finisher of our faith is through the promise of eternal life. In *John 11:25-26*, Jesus states, *"I am the resurrection and the life. He who believes in Me, though he may die, he shall live. And whoever lives and believes in Me shall never die."* These words remind us that our faith journey does not end with our earthly lives but continues into eternity as we are reunited with Jesus and experience the fullness of God's love and presence.

Throughout my life, I have experienced numerous

instances of Jesus' role as the Finisher of my faith. During times of doubt, fear, or discouragement, I have often turned to the words of Scripture and the example of Jesus' own life to find strength and hope. Time and again, I have been reminded of the steadfast love and faithfulness of Jesus, who never abandons us but continually guides and refines us on our spiritual journey.

As we reflect on the role of Jesus as the Author and Finisher of our faith, it is important to remember that our faith journey is not a static, one-time event but rather an ongoing process of growth and transformation. In the words of the Apostle Peter, *"Grow in the grace and knowledge of our Lord and Savior Jesus Christ" (2 Peter 3:18).* By continually seeking to deepen our relationship with Jesus and striving to follow His example, we can experience the fullness of life and purpose that He offers us.

Recognizing Jesus as the Author and Finisher of our faith is essential for developing a strong and vibrant spiritual life. As the foundation of our faith, Jesus initiates our relationship with God and guides us through the challenges and joys of our spiritual journey. By embracing His role as the Author and Finisher of our faith, we can experience the transformative power of His love and grace and ultimately come to know the fullness of God's purpose for our lives.

I once heard a humorous story that, in a way, demonstrated the transformative power of Jesus in a believer's life. He explained that before he became a Christian, he had a terrible habit of losing his temper and using foul language.

One day, after a particularly heated exchange with a coworker, he prayed fervently, *"Lord, please help me control my tongue and my temper. I need Your guidance to be more Christ-like in my words and actions."* As he prayed, he suddenly had a humorous thought. *"Lord, if You could help Moses part the Red Sea, surely You can help me part with my foul language!"*

The room erupted in laughter, but the story also served as a reminder of the transformative power of Jesus in our lives. No matter our struggles or weaknesses, we can turn to Jesus as the Author and Finisher of our faith, trusting that He will guide us in our journey toward spiritual growth and transformation.

In this book, we will explore various aspects of our faith journey with Jesus, examining the role of the Holy Spirit, the importance of the Christian community, and the practice of spiritual disciplines. As we delve deeper into these topics, may we find encouragement and inspiration in the knowledge that Jesus is the Author and Finisher of our faith, the one who initiates, sustains, and completes our spiritual journey with unwavering love and grace.

2

THE COMPANION
The Role of the Holy Spirit in Our Faith Journey

As we continue to explore the various aspects of our faith journey, it is essential to consider the role of the Holy Spirit, the divine companion who accompanies and empowers us as we grow in our relationship with God. We will examine the function and significance of the Holy Spirit in our spiritual journey, drawing from Scripture and personal experiences to illuminate the transformative power of the Spirit in our lives.

The Holy Spirit is an integral part of the Christian faith, serving as the third person of the Holy Trinity, along with God the Father and Jesus Christ the Son. Jesus Himself spoke about the importance of the Holy Spirit during His earthly ministry, promising His disciples that He would send the Spirit to be with them after His ascension. In *John 14:16-17*, Jesus says, *"And I will pray the Father, and He will give you another Helper, that He may abide with you forever—the Spirit of truth, whom the world cannot receive because it neither sees Him nor knows Him; but you know Him, for He dwells with you and will be in you."*

The arrival of the Holy Spirit was dramatically demonstrated on the day of Pentecost, as described in Acts 2. The disciples were gathered together in Jerusalem when a sound like a rushing wind suddenly filled the room, and tongues of fire appeared, resting on each of them. Filled with the Holy Spirit, the disciples began to speak in other languages, proclaiming the wonders of God to those gathered in the city. This miraculous event marked the birth of the Christian Church and the beginning of the Holy Spirit's active presence in the lives of believers.

The Holy Spirit plays several crucial roles in our faith journey, one of which is serving as our divine teacher and guide. Jesus promised that the Holy Spirit would lead His followers into all truth, helping them to understand and apply the teachings of Scripture *(John 16:13)*. As we study the Bible and seek to grow in our faith, the Holy Spirit illuminates our minds and hearts, revealing the wisdom and knowledge contained within its pages.

I recall a time when I was struggling to understand a particular passage in Scripture. Despite reading the verses multiple times, I felt perplexed by their meaning. As I prayed for guidance and understanding, I experienced a sudden moment of clarity, as if the Holy Spirit had opened my eyes to the truth hidden within the text. This experience reinforced my belief in the Holy Spirit's role as a divine teacher, guiding and instructing me as I delve deeper into God's Word.

Another vital function of the Holy Spirit is empowering and equipping believers for service and ministry. In *Acts 1:8,* Jesus states, *"But you shall receive power when the Holy Spirit has come upon you; and you shall be witnesses to Me in Jerusalem, and in all Judea and Samaria, and to the end of the earth."* The Holy Spirit not only imparts spiritual gifts to believers but also provides the strength and courage needed to share the gospel with others and fulfill the Great Commission *(Matthew 28:19-20).*

My most memorable experience with the Holy Spirit occurred while sharing my faith. I felt inadequate and unprepared to share my faith, but I prayed for the Holy Spirit's guidance and strength. I found boldness and conviction as the Spirit worked through me to touch the hearts of those I encountered. This experience taught me the importance of relying on the Holy Spirit's power and presence in my life, especially when facing challenges.

In addition to guiding and empowering us, the Holy Spirit provides comfort and reassurance in our faith journey. Jesus referred to the Holy Spirit as the *"Comforter"* or

"Helper" (John 14:26), promising that the Spirit would provide solace and support to His followers in times of need. During moments of doubt, fear, or sorrow, the Holy Spirit offers a comforting presence, reminding us of God's love, faithfulness, and care.

There was a period in my life when I experienced overwhelming feelings of grief, pain, and loss. In those dark moments, I turned to prayer, seeking the comfort and strength of the Holy Spirit. As I prayed, I felt a sense of peace and assurance that could only be attributed to the Holy Spirit's comforting presence, reminding me that God was with me in the midst of my pain and sorrow.

Finally, the Holy Spirit plays a crucial role in sanctification, the ongoing transformation of believers into the image of Christ. As we grow in our faith and deepen our relationship with God, the Holy Spirit works within us to refine our character and empower us to obey God's will. The Apostle Paul writes in *Galatians 5:22-23, "But the fruit of the Spirit is love, joy, peace, longsuffering, kindness, goodness, faithfulness, gentleness, self-control."* Through the indwelling presence of the Holy Spirit, we are enabled to develop and exhibit these Christ-like qualities in our lives.

I have seen the sanctifying work of the Holy Spirit in my own life, as He has gently but persistently guided me in the ongoing process of spiritual growth and transformation. As I have yielded to the Spirit's leading, I have witnessed the development of patience, love, and humility within my character – qualities that I know result from the Holy Spirit's work in me.

The Holy Spirit is an essential companion on our faith journey, guiding, empowering, comforting, and sanctifying us as we grow in our relationship with God.

By cultivating an awareness of the Holy Spirit's presence in our lives and seeking His guidance and support, we can experience the transformative power of God's love and grace in new and profound ways.

A New Beginning

While writing this book and being forced to relive the pain of when I was a little girl, the birthday tragedy taught me valuable lessons about perseverance, faith, and resilience. These lessons can help us when we face trials and tribulations.

Perseverance Through Adversity

In the face of seemingly insurmountable odds, I refused to give up. Despite the pain and the struggle, I fought to regain my ability to walk. This unwavering perseverance is something I hope you can learn from. When faced with our own struggles, it's important to remember that giving up should never be an option. We must keep pushing forward, even when the odds seem stacked against us.

The Power of Faith

Faith played a crucial role in my recovery as a young girl. My belief in God and the unwavering support of my family gave me the strength to overcome the challenges I faced. In your own life, faith can be a powerful driving force. Whether faith in God, ourselves, or the people around you, believing in something greater can help you push through your struggles and emerge victorious.

Resilience and Learning from Experiences

I didn't just overcome my physical challenges as a young girl and learned valuable lessons from the experiences. I understood the importance of standing up after a fall and the value of each new day. You, too, can learn from your good and bad experiences. By embracing resilience and learning from your struggles, you can grow and become better prepared for whatever life may throw at you.

3

EMBRACING THE WORST-CASE SCENARIO
The Power of Scripture and Faith in Adversity

Our legs are pivotal and one of the most important parts of our bodies. Losing one's leg can leave a physical and er scar that will disable the individual for life. When I almost lost my legs, I remember the fear that washed over my soul and the pain I felt. But one of the ways Jesus helped me was the ability to embrace my fears and confront my challenges head-on.

Facing Our Fears

I faced the prospect of losing my legs – a terrifying thought for anyone.

Yet, my family and I didn't shy away from the situation. Instead, my parents sought help and advice, ultimately finding a solution that saved my legs. It's important to face our fears rather than run from them. By confronting our challenges directly, we give ourselves the best chance of finding solutions and overcoming adversity.

The Importance of Support

The support of family, friends, and medical professionals played a crucial role in my recovery. Without the help and encouragement of those around me, I may not have been able to push through my pain and regain my ability to walk. In your own life, you should never underestimate the value of support. Whether it's from loved ones, friends, or professionals, having a strong support system can make all the difference when facing adversity.

The Miracle of Hope

I never lost hope when faced with the idea of losing my legs. I believed in my ability to walk again, even when the odds seemed stacked against me. This unwavering hope and belief in the face of adversity is something you can all learn from. Even in your darkest moments, maintaining hope strengthens and motivates you to keep fighting for a better tomorrow.

The journey through life is never without its storms. As I faced the challenges of adversity, I found solace and strength in the scriptures. As a person of faith, I discovered that the wisdom and guidance found within the pages of the Bible provided an anchor amid my struggles. In this chapter, I will share some of the most profound scriptures that helped me through my darkest moments and how they can be a source of strength and inspiration for anyone going through difficult times.

One of my favorite scriptures is *Isaiah 40:31*, which reads, *"But those who hope in the Lord will renew their strength. They will soar on wings like eagles; they will run and not grow weary; they will walk and not be faint."* This verse reminded me that placing my hope in God would give me the strength to endure the trials ahead. It also assured me that I was not alone in my struggle, as God was with me every step of the way.

Another powerful scripture I held close to my heart during my times of adversity is *Romans 8:28: "And we know that in all things God works for the good of those who love him, who have been called according to his purpose."* This verse reminded me that no matter how bleak or challenging my situation, God worked behind the scenes to bring about a greater good. It gave me the hope that my suffering was not in vain and would ultimately lead to something positive and meaningful.

One of the most challenging aspects of facing adversity is feeling overwhelmed and consumed by our burdens. *Psalm 55:22* offers comfort in these moments: *"Cast your cares on the Lord, and he will sustain you; he will never let the righteous be shaken."* This Scripture reminded me to let go of my worries and fears and place them in God's capable hands. By doing so, I found a sense of peace and calm in the storm.

In moments of intense struggle, I found immense comfort in the words of Jesus in *Matthew 11:28-30: "Come to me, all you who are weary and burdened, and I will give you rest. Take my yoke upon you and learn from me, for I am gentle and humble in heart, and you will find rest for your souls. For my yoke is easy, and my burden is light."* These words served as an invitation for me to surrender my struggles and pain to Jesus and to trust in His ability to carry my burdens.

One of the most powerful scriptures that helped me maintain my faith during adversity is *Hebrews 11:1: "Now faith is confidence in what we hope for and assurance about what we do not see."* This verse reminded me of the importance of having unwavering faith during my trials. I learned to trust in God's plan, even when I could not see the outcome or understand the reasons behind my suffering.

Throughout my journey, I found it helpful to surround myself with the support of loved ones who shared my faith. We often turn to the words of *1 Thessalonians 5:11: "Therefore encourage one another and build each other up, just as in fact you are doing."* In the darkest moments, the encouragement and support of my friends and family were invaluable in helping me find the strength to keep moving forward.

In moments of despair, I would turn to the words of *Psalm 46:1-3: "God is our refuge and strength, an ever-present help in trouble. Therefore we will not fear, though the earth give way and the mountains fall into the heart of the sea, though its waters roar and foam and the mountains quake with their surging."* This Scripture reminded me that even when the world around me seemed to be crumbling, God was still my refuge and source of strength. His presence was a constant reassurance, giving me the courage to face my fears and continue my journey.

Another vital scripture I relied on during adversity is *Philippians 4:13: "I can do all things through Christ who strengthens me."* This verse was a powerful reminder that I had the strength to overcome any obstacle with Christ by my side. As I faced the trials and tribulations of life, I would repeat this Scripture as a mantra, drawing strength from the knowledge that Christ was empowering me to persevere.

During the most challenging moments, when I felt

as though I was at the end of my rope, I would find solace in the words of *2 Corinthians 12:9:* *"But he said to me, 'My grace is sufficient for you, for my power is made perfect in weakness.' Therefore I will boast all the more gladly about my weaknesses so that Christ's power may rest on me."* In my weakest moments, I found strength in my faith, embracing my vulnerability and allowing Christ's power to work through me.

As I reflect on my journey through adversity, I am reminded of the words of *James 1:2-4:* *"Consider it pure joy, my brothers and sisters, whenever you face trials of many kinds, because you know that the testing of your faith produces perseverance. Let perseverance finish its work so that you may be mature and complete, not lacking anything."* This Scripture taught me that my trials were not merely random or senseless suffering but opportunities to grow and strengthen my faith.

In the midst of adversity, I found it helpful to meditate on the words of *Psalm 23*, which provided a vivid reminder of God's love and care for me: *"The Lord is my shepherd, I lack nothing. He makes me lie down in green pastures, he leads me beside quiet waters, he refreshes my soul. He guides me along the right paths for his name's sake. Even though I walk through the darkest valley, I will fear no evil, for you are with me; your rod and your staff, they comfort me."*

The power of Scripture is undeniable, and the verses I have shared here are a small sampling of the countless passages that can provide solace, strength, and guidance during times of adversity.

By immersing myself in the Word of God and drawing upon my faith, I found the resilience and courage to navigate even the most challenging moments of my journey.

I encourage you, dear reader, to turn to the scriptures when you need strength, hope, or guidance. Allow the Word of God to be a lamp unto your feet and a light unto your path *(Psalm 119:105)*, and trust in the Lord with all your heart *(Proverbs 3:5)*. With faith as your anchor; you too can overcome the storms of life and emerge stronger, more resilient, and more deeply rooted in your faith.

4

FAITH AS A GUIDING FORCE

Finding Purpose in the Midst of Struggle

During my struggles, I often questioned the purpose of my suffering. Why was I facing these challenges, and what could I learn from them? During these moments, I turned to the scriptures, seeking answers and a deeper understanding of God's plan for me.

One of the most profound and comforting scriptures I encountered while questioning was *Romans 8:28: "And we know that in all things God works for the good of those who love him, who have been called according to his purpose."* This verse reassured me that despite my struggles, God was working to bring about something good. It reminded me that my trials were not meaningless but were, in fact, part of a larger divine plan.

Another scripture that helped me find purpose in my suffering was *1 Peter 4:12-13: "Dear friends, do not be surprised at the fiery ordeal that has come on you to test you, as though something strange was happening to you.*

But rejoice inasmuch as you participate in the sufferings of Christ, so that you may be overjoyed when his glory is revealed." This passage taught me that my suffering was not only an opportunity to grow in faith and perseverance and a means of participating in Christ's own suffering. Through my trials, I was able to share in the redemptive work of Jesus and find a more profound sense of meaning and purpose.

In seeking to understand the purpose behind my struggles, I also found solace in the words of *2 Corinthians 1:3-4:* *"Praise be to the God and Father of our Lord Jesus Christ, the Father of compassion and the God of all comfort, who comforts us in all our troubles so that we can comfort those in any trouble with the comfort we receive from God."* This Scripture revealed that one of the purposes of my suffering was to enable me to empathize with and support others facing similar struggles. In this way, my trials became a source of strength and healing for myself and those around me.

As I continued to search the scriptures for understanding, I was struck by the words of Isaiah in *Isaiah 43:2: "When you pass through the waters, I will be with you; and when you pass through the rivers, they will not sweep over you. When you walk through the fire, you will not be burned; the flames will not set you ablaze."* This verse served as a powerful reminder that God was with me through every trial, providing protection and guidance even in the most challenging circumstances.

In my quest for purpose, I also found inspiration in the story of Joseph, as recounted in the book of Genesis. Joseph's life was marked by a series of trials and tribulations, from being sold into slavery by his own brothers to being falsely accused and imprisoned. Yet, despite these hardships, Joseph remained faithful to God and ultimately rose to a place of power and influence.

As *Genesis 50:20* reveals, Joseph understood that his suffering had a purpose: *"You intended to harm me, but God intended it for good to accomplish what is now being done, the saving of many lives."* Joseph's story taught me that even in the midst of great suffering, God can bring about incredible good.

One of the most powerful scriptures that helped me find purpose in my struggles was *Jeremiah 29:11: "For I know the plans I have for you,"* declares the Lord, "plans to prosper you and not to harm you, plans to give you hope and a future." This verse reassured me that despite my trials, God had a plan for my life – a plan marked by hope, prosperity, and a promise-filled future.

Throughout my journey, I have also found great comfort in the words of Jesus as recorded in *Matthew*

11:28-30: "Come to me, all you who are weary and burdened, and I will give you rest. Take my yoke upon you and learn from me, for I am gentle and humble in heart, and you will find rest for your souls. For my yoke is easy, and my burden is light." This Scripture has reminded me that even during my struggles, I can find rest and solace in Jesus, who understands and shares in my suffering.

Another passage that has comforted me during difficult times is *Philippians 4:6-7: "Do not be anxious about anything, but in every situation, by prayer and petition, with thanksgiving, present your requests to God. And the peace of God, which transcends all understanding, will guard your hearts and your minds in Christ Jesus."* Through prayer and reliance on God, I have experienced a peace that surpasses human understanding, even during life's most challenging moments.

As I have journeyed through my struggles, I have come to understand that my trials are not without purpose. The scriptures have taught me that through suffering, I can grow in faith, participate in the redemptive work of Christ, and become a source of comfort and support to others facing similar challenges.

Moreover, I have learned that God is always with me, guiding and protecting me through every trial and tribulation.

As you face your struggles, I encourage you to read the Scriptures for guidance, comfort, and inspiration. Immerse yourself in the words of God and allow them to shape your understanding of your trials and your place in His divine plan. Remember the promise of *Romans 8:18:* *"I consider that our present sufferings are not worth comparing with the glory that will be revealed in us."*

In my life, faith played a significant role in helping me overcome my challenges. My faith in God and myself gave me strength and determination. In the face of adversity, finding strength and motivation to keep moving forward is important. Life is filled with challenges, and overcoming these challenges makes us stronger and more resilient. In my story, the challenges I faced were extreme, but they allowed me to grow and develop as a person.

I have come to realize that while the road of life is often marked by pain and struggle, these challenges are not without meaning. Through the scriptures and a deepening relationship with God, I have discovered a sense of purpose in my suffering.

My prayer for you, dear reader, is that you, too, may find comfort, strength, and purpose in the words of the Bible as you navigate the trials and tribulations of your own life. May the peace of God be with you always, and may you find hope and solace in the knowledge that you

Elizabeth Olufemi

are not alone in your journey.

5
CULTIVATING A HEART OF GRATITUDE

In my walk with God, I have learned that cultivating a heart of gratitude is essential to spiritual growth. Gratitude shifts our focus from our problems and challenges to the goodness and blessings of God. It reminds us that even in the midst of our difficulties, God is at work in our lives, providing for our needs and equipping us with the strength and resources necessary to face the challenges before us.

One of the most powerful passages of Scripture that have helped me to develop a heart of gratitude is *1 Thessalonians 5:16-18: "Rejoice always, pray continually, give thanks in all circumstances; for this is God's will for you in Christ Jesus."* This passage encourages us to rejoice and give thanks in all situations, recognizing that our gratitude depends not on our external circumstances but on our relationship with God and our trust in His goodness.

In my own life, I have found that developing a heart

of gratitude has required me to shift my perspective and focus on the ways God has been at work in my life, even in the midst of trials and hardships. This has involved intentional reflection on the blessings I have received and the ways in which God has provided for me and my family. As I have made a conscious effort to practice gratitude, I have noticed a profound shift in my attitude and outlook on life.

The scriptures are filled with examples of individuals who demonstrated a heart of gratitude despite their difficult circumstances. One such example is the apostle Paul, who wrote these words to the Philippians while imprisoned and facing an uncertain future: *"I have learned to be content whatever the circumstances. I know what it is to be in need, and I know what it is to have plenty. I have learned the secret of being content in any and every situation, whether well-fed or hungry, whether living in plenty or in want. I can do all this through him who gives me strength" (Philippians 4:11-13).*

Paul's example reminds us that gratitude and contentment are not dependent on our circumstances but rather on our reliance on God and our confidence in His goodness and provision.

Another powerful passage that has helped me cultivate a heart of gratitude is *Psalm 103:1-5: "Praise the*

Lord, my soul; all my inmost being, praise his holy name. Praise the Lord, my soul, and forget not all his benefits— who forgives all your sins and heals all your diseases, who redeems your life from the pit and crowns you with love and compassion, who satisfies your desires with good things so that your youth is renewed like the eagle's." This psalm encourages us to remember and reflect on the many blessings and benefits we have received from God and to respond with heartfelt praise and gratitude.

To cultivate a heart of gratitude, it is important to develop regular practices that help us to focus on God's goodness and provision. One practice that has been particularly helpful for me is keeping a gratitude journal. Each day, I take a few moments to write down at least three things for which I am grateful. This practice has helped me to become more aware of God's presence and provision in my life and has fostered a more profound sense of gratitude and contentment.

Another helpful practice is engaging in regular prayer and thanksgiving. As we spend time in prayer, we can express our gratitude to God for His many blessings and ask for His help in maintaining a grateful heart. The scriptures encourage us in this practice, as we read in *Colossians 4:2:* *"Devote yourselves to prayer, being watchful and thankful."*

Cultivating a heart of gratitude within our families and communities is also important. We can do this by sharing our gratitude with others and encouraging them to do the same. One way to facilitate this is by setting aside time during family meals or gatherings to share what each person is thankful for. This practice not only fosters a sense of gratitude but also strengthens our relationships with one another as we recognize and celebrate God's work in our lives.

Moreover, we can express our gratitude by serving others and giving back to our communities. As we use our time, talents, and resources to help those in need, we are living out our gratitude for God's blessings in our lives. In doing so, we also follow the example of Jesus, who *"came not to be served, but to serve"* (Mark 10:45).

One of the most profound experiences of gratitude I have had occurred during a mission trip to a developing country. As I witnessed the deep faith and gratitude of people with so little material possessions, I was humbled and challenged to reevaluate my perspective on gratitude. This experience served as a powerful reminder that true gratitude transcends our circumstances and is rooted in our relationship with God.

The scriptures provide ample encouragement for cultivating a heart of gratitude. In Psalm 136, the psalmist repeatedly proclaims, "Give thanks to the Lord, for he is good. His love endures forever." This refrain serves as a reminder of God's unchanging goodness and love, which are always worthy of our gratitude.

Additionally, the apostle Paul reminds us in *Ephesians 5:19-20, "Speak to one another with psalms, hymns, and songs from the Spirit. Sing and make music from your heart to the Lord, always giving thanks to God the Father for everything, in the name of our Lord Jesus Christ."* In this passage, Paul highlights the importance of communal expressions of gratitude and worship and the vital role gratitude plays in our relationship with God.

Cultivating a heart of gratitude is essential to our spiritual growth and well-being. As we intentionally focus on God's goodness and provision, practice regular habits of gratitude, and express our gratitude to others, we will experience a more profound sense of joy, contentment, and peace. Ultimately, a heart of gratitude enables us to recognize better and respond to God's presence and work in our lives, drawing us closer to Him and equipping us to be a blessing to others.

"Let the peace of Christ rule in your hearts, since as members of one body you were called to peace. And be thankful. Let the message of Christ dwell among you richly as you teach and admonish one another with all wisdom

through psalms, hymns, and songs from the Spirit, singing to God with gratitude in your hearts. And whatever you do, whether in Word or deed, do it all in the name of the Lord Jesus, giving thanks to God the Father through him." (Colossians 3:15-17)

6

THE ONGOING PROJECT
Growing in Faith through Life's Challenges

The Christian journey is a lifelong pursuit marked by periods of growth, trials, and transformation. Our faith is continually tested and refined as we navigate life's challenges. However, through these challenges, we can grow closer to God and deepen our understanding of His love and grace. We will explore the importance of cultivating a resilient faith, using biblical teachings and personal reflections to provide encouragement and guidance when we face life's obstacles.

One of the most powerful passages on the subject of trials and faith can be found in *James 1:2-4*, where the Apostle James writes, *"Consider it pure joy, my brothers and sisters, whenever you face trials of many kinds, because you know that the testing of your faith produces perseverance. Let perseverance finish its work so that you may be mature and complete, not lacking anything."* These words remind us that trials are an essential part of our spiritual growth, refining our faith and molding us into the image of Christ.

As we face various challenges, we must remember that God is always with us, providing strength and guidance. *Isaiah 41:10* offers reassurance, stating, *"So do not fear, for I am with you; do not be dismayed, for I am your God. I will strengthen you and help you; I will uphold you with my righteous right hand."* In times of difficulty, we can find solace in knowing that God is our constant companion, walking alongside us and equipping us with the resources we need to overcome adversity.

Personal Reflection: A few years ago, I faced a significant health challenge that left me feeling vulnerable and fearful. During this time, I clung to the promises found in Scripture and relied on the support and encouragement of my faith community. As I navigated the physical and emotional challenges of my illness, I was reminded of Paul's words in *2 Corinthians 12:9, "But he said to me, 'My grace is sufficient for you, for my power is made perfect in weakness.'*

Therefore, I will boast all the more gladly about my weaknesses, so that Christ's power may rest on me." Through this experience, I learned to rely on God's strength and discovered a deeper understanding of His faithfulness and love.

In addition to leaning on God's strength, we can

also find comfort and encouragement in the stories of biblical figures who faced challenges and grew in their faith. Consider the story of Abraham, who demonstrated great faith when asked to sacrifice his son Isaac *(Genesis 22:1-19)*. Despite the enormity of the request, Abraham trusted God and was willing to obey, even in the face of immense personal loss. As a result, his faith was credited to him as righteousness *(Romans 4:3)*.

Another example can be found in the life of Joseph, who was sold into slavery by his brothers and later imprisoned on false charges *(Genesis 37-50)*. Despite these trials, Joseph remained faithful to God and ultimately rose to a position of power in Egypt, where he was able to save his family from famine. His story demonstrates the power of perseverance, faith in hardship, and God's ability to use our trials for His purposes.

As we encounter various challenges throughout our lives, staying connected to God through prayer, worship, and studying His Word is essential. In *Ephesians 6:10-11*, Paul exhorts believers to *"be strong in the Lord and his mighty power. Put on the full armor of God so that you can take your stand against the devil's schemes."* By remaining grounded in our faith, we can confidently face life's obstacles, knowing God works in us and through us.

One way to strengthen our faith and grow in our

relationship with God is to cultivate an attitude of gratitude. In *1 Thessalonians 5:16-18*, Paul writes, *"Rejoice always, pray continually, give thanks in all circumstances; for this is God's will for you in Christ Jesus."* By expressing gratitude for our blessings, we can develop a deeper appreciation for God's presence in our lives and maintain a hopeful perspective amid trials.

Personal Reflection: During a challenging season, I began keeping a gratitude journal, recording at least three things each day for which I was thankful. This simple practice helped me focus on the positive aspects of my life and reminded me of God's faithfulness, even amid struggle. Reflecting on the many ways God had blessed me, I found my faith growing stronger and my trust in His plan deepening.

Another critical aspect of growing in faith through life's challenges is the support and encouragement of fellow believers. In *Hebrews 10:24-25*, we are reminded of the value of Christian community: *"And let us consider how we may spur one another on toward love and good deeds, not giving up meeting together, as some are in the habit of doing, but encouraging one another—and all the more as you see the Day approaching."* By sharing our struggles, triumphs, and insights with others, we can foster a sense of unity and strengthen our collective faith.

Personal Reflection: I have been blessed with a strong network of Christian friends who have been instrumental in my faith journey. Through our shared experiences, prayer, and mutual support, we have grown together in understanding God's love and grace. When faced with challenges, I know I can rely on this community for encouragement and guidance, helping me remain steadfast in my faith.

Growing in faith through life's challenges is an ongoing project, requiring us to continually seek God's wisdom, strength, and guidance. By embracing trials as opportunities for growth, staying connected to God through prayer and Scripture, cultivating gratitude, and leaning on the support of fellow believers, we can develop a resilient faith that not only sustains us in difficult times but also enables us to be a source of strength and encouragement for others.

As we press on in our journey, let us hold onto the words of *Philippians 3:12-14:* *"Not that I have already obtained all this, or have already arrived at my goal, but I press on to take hold of that for which Christ Jesus took hold of me. Brothers and sisters, I do not consider myself yet to have taken hold of it. But one thing I do: Forgetting what is behind and straining toward what is ahead, I press on toward the goal to win the prize for which God has*

Elizabeth Olufemi

called me heavenward in Christ Jesus."

7

SPIRITUAL DISCIPLINES
Tools for Building a Stronger Faith

Spiritual disciplines are essential practices that help us develop and maintain a close relationship with God, leading to a stronger faith. These disciplines, practiced by Christians throughout history, can provide a solid foundation for spiritual growth and maturity. This chapter will explore several key spiritual disciplines, including prayer, Bible study, meditation, fasting, and service, and how they can be integrated into our daily lives.

Prayer is the most fundamental spiritual discipline, providing us with a direct line of communication with God. In *1 Thessalonians 5:17*, we are encouraged to *"pray continually,"* emphasizing the importance of maintaining an ongoing dialogue with God. Through prayer, we express our love, gratitude, and concerns to God and open our hearts to receive His guidance, wisdom, and peace.

Personal Reflection: Prayer has been an essential part of my faith journey. Over the years, I have found that setting aside a specific time each day for focused prayer helps me stay connected to God, even during busy or challenging periods. This dedicated prayer time allows me to express my thoughts and feelings to God while listening to His gentle voice guiding me.

Bible study is another crucial spiritual discipline that equips us with knowledge and understanding of God's Word. Regular engagement with Scripture helps us grow in our relationship with God and learn more about His character, promises, and plan for our lives. *2 Timothy 3:16-17* states, *"All Scripture is God-breathed and is useful for teaching, rebuking, correcting and training in righteousness, so that the servant of God may be thoroughly equipped for every good work."*

Personal Reflection: Studying the Bible has been transformative for me. As I delve into the stories, teachings, and wisdom of Scripture, I gain a deeper understanding of God's love and grace. By reflecting on Scripture passages and applying them to my life, I find that my faith and trust in God continue to grow.

Meditation is a spiritual discipline that involves quieting our minds and focusing our thoughts on God, often through contemplation of a specific Scripture passage or spiritual truth. *Psalm 1:1-2* highlights the importance of meditating on God's Word: *"Blessed is the one...whose delight is in the law of the Lord, and who meditates on his law day and night."* Meditation enables us to connect more deeply with God and His Word, leading to spiritual growth and strengthened faith.

Personal Reflection: Practicing meditation has profoundly impacted my spiritual life. Setting aside time to quiet my mind and focus on God's Word makes me more attuned to the Holy Spirit's guidance and more aware of God's presence in my life. Meditation has also helped me develop a greater sense of peace and inner calm, even during life's challenges.

Fasting is the voluntary abstinence from food or other activities for a specific period to focus on prayer and spiritual growth. Fasting allows us to prioritize our relationship with God over our physical needs and desires, leading to a deeper dependence on Him. Jesus himself modeled the importance of fasting when He fasted for forty days in the wilderness *(Matthew 4:1-11)*.

Personal Reflection: I have found fasting to be a powerful tool for deepening my faith and drawing closer to God. When I choose to fast from food or other activities, I am reminded of my dependence on God for sustenance and strength. This intentional focus on God helps me to grow in my understanding of His character and to develop a greater appreciation for His provision in my life.

Service is a spiritual discipline that involves using our time, talents, and resources to meet the needs of others in the name of Christ. Jesus emphasized the importance of service when He said, *"Truly I tell you, whatever you did for one of the least of these brothers and sisters of mine, you did for me" (Matthew 25:40)*. Serving others not only demonstrates God's love to those in need but also helps us develop a Christ-like attitude of humility and compassion.

Personal Reflection: I have experienced the power of service in my own life as a means of growing in faith. I have witnessed God's love in action through volunteering at my local church, participating in mission trips, and helping those in need within my community. Serving others has also been a catalyst for spiritual growth, as I am continually challenged to step outside my comfort zone and rely on God for guidance and strength.

Spiritual disciplines are essential for strengthening faith and deepening our relationship with God. By engaging in prayer, Bible study, meditation, fasting, and service, we can grow in our understanding of God's character and His plan for our lives. By making these disciplines a consistent part of our daily lives, we can experience the joy, peace, and spiritual growth that come from a vibrant, intimate relationship with our Creator.

Personal Reflection: Reflecting on my faith journey,

I am grateful for the spiritual disciplines that have helped me grow closer to God. These practices have been essential in deepening my faith, providing a solid foundation for my relationship with the Lord. As I continue to engage in these disciplines, I am excited to see how God will use them to transform my life and equip me for the work He has called me to do.

Let us be encouraged to pursue these spiritual disciplines with dedication and perseverance, knowing they will lead to a deeper relationship with God and a more vibrant faith. And as we practice these disciplines, let us always remember the words of *Hebrews 12:1-2, "And let us run with perseverance the race marked out for us, fixing our eyes on Jesus, the pioneer and perfecter of faith."*

8

JESUS AS THE FINISHER
The Promise of Eternal Life

One of the most beautiful promises in the Bible is the assurance of eternal life for those who put their faith in Jesus Christ. Throughout the New Testament, we find passages that speak of the hope and joy that await us in eternity. As we grow in faith and draw closer to Jesus, we can look forward to the day we will be with Him forever.

John 3:16, one of the most well-known verses in the Bible, provides a clear and concise summary of the gospel message: *"For God so loved the world that he gave his one and only Son, that whoever believes in him shall not perish but have eternal life."* This verse not only affirms God's immense love for us but also reveals the gift of eternal life available to all who believe in Jesus.

Personal Reflection: I still remember the moment I first understood the meaning of *John 3:16*. As I read those words, I was struck by God's incredible love and grace. The promise of eternal life became real to me, and

Author and Finisher

I realized that by trusting in Jesus, I could have a personal relationship with God and look forward to spending eternity with Him.

Jesus promised eternal life to those who believe in Him and demonstrated His power over death through His own resurrection. In *John 11:25-26,* Jesus says, *"I am the resurrection and the life. The one who believes in me will live, even though they die; and whoever lives by believing in me will never die."* Through His resurrection, Jesus conquered death and guaranteed our eternal life with Him.

As we face various trials and challenges in our lives, the promise of eternal life provides a source of comfort and hope. In *Romans 8:18*, the Apostle Paul writes, *"I consider that our present sufferings are not worth comparing with the glory that will be revealed in us."* The trials we face in this life are temporary, but the joy and peace we will experience in eternity are beyond compare.

Personal Reflection: I have experienced moments of doubt and struggle throughout my faith journey. During those times, I have often turned to the promise of eternal life as a source of encouragement and hope. Knowing that I have a future with Jesus in heaven has helped me to endure difficult times and keep pressing forward in faith.

The Bible also speaks of the transformation that will occur in eternity. In *1 Corinthians 15:51-52*, Paul writes,

"Listen, I tell you a mystery: We will not all sleep, but we will all be changed—in a flash, in the twinkling of an eye, at the last trumpet. For the trumpet will sound, the dead will be raised imperishable, and we will be changed." This passage reveals that when Jesus returns, our mortal bodies will be transformed into immortal, glorified bodies free from sin and decay.

Personal Reflection: The promise of our future transformation is a source of great anticipation for me. I look forward to the day when I will be free from the limitations and struggles of this earthly body and will be able to fully enjoy the presence of God in my glorified body.

As we grow in our faith and walk with Jesus, we must keep our eyes fixed on the promise of eternal life. *Hebrews 12:2* encourages us to fix our eyes on Jesus, *"the pioneer and perfecter of faith,"* who endured the cross for the joy set before Him. The same joy that motivated Jesus to endure the cross is the joy that awaits us in eternity.

Personal Reflection: I have found that keeping my focus on the promise of eternal life profoundly impacts my daily walk with Jesus. When I remember the eternal perspective, I can endure life's challenges and keep my faith strong. The hope of eternity with Jesus gives me the strength and motivation to persevere in my spiritual journey, no matter the obstacles I face.

In *Revelation 21:4*, we are given a glimpse of the beauty and joy that await us in eternity: *"He will wipe every tear from their eyes. There will be no more death or mourning or crying or pain, for the old order of things has passed away."* This passage provides a powerful reminder that our trials are temporary and a glorious future awaits us in heaven.

Personal Reflection: As I reflect on the promise of eternal life, I am overwhelmed by the love and grace of God. The thought of spending eternity in the presence of my Savior, free from the pain and suffering of this world, fills my heart with joy and gratitude.

As followers of Jesus, we have been given the incredible gift of eternal life, and this promise should shape the way we live our lives. In *Titus 2:11-13*, we are reminded of the impact that the hope of eternity should have on our daily lives: *"For the grace of God has appeared that offers salvation to all people. It teaches us to say 'No' to ungodliness and worldly passions, and to live self-controlled, upright and godly lives in this present age, while we wait for the blessed hope—the appearing of the glory of our great God and Savior, Jesus Christ."*

Personal Reflection: Keeping the promise of eternal life in mind profoundly impacts my choices and priorities.

It helps me resist temptation and choose to live a life that is pleasing to God, knowing that my true reward lies in eternity with Jesus.

As we grow in our faith and deepen our relationship with Jesus, let us cling to the promise of eternal life, allowing it to motivate and encourage us in our daily walk. May we fix our eyes on Jesus, the Finisher of our faith, as we eagerly anticipate the day we will be with Him forever in eternity.

Personal Reflection: As I reflect on my faith journey, I am incredibly grateful for the promise of eternal life. It has been a source of comfort, hope, and strength in the face of life's challenges. As I continue to grow closer to Jesus, I eagerly anticipate the day I will be with Him forever in heaven, experiencing the fullness of joy and peace that He has promised.

9

THE MASTERPIECE
Living a Life of Purpose and Impact

Throughout my journey of faith, I have come to understand that God has a unique and specific purpose for each of us. He has designed us as His masterpiece, created for good works that He has planned for us to do *(Ephesians 2:10)*. By discovering and embracing our God-given purpose, we can live a life of impact, making a difference in the world around us.

Personal Reflection: *As I have grown in my relationship with Jesus, I have experienced the joy and fulfillment of aligning my life with God's purpose. I have seen firsthand how living with purpose can transform not only my life but also those around me.*

Understanding our purpose begins with recognizing that we were created by God and for God. As *Psalm 139:13-14* says, *"For you created my inmost being; you knit me together in my mother's womb. I praise you because I am fearfully and wonderfully made; your works are wonderful, I know that full well."* We are not accidents or the result of chance; we are intentionally designed by our Creator, who knows us intimately and loves us deeply.

Personal Reflection: Reflecting on the truth that I am fearfully and wonderfully made has filled me with awe and gratitude. It has helped me see my worth and value through God's eyes and motivated me to pursue the purpose for which I was created.

As we seek to discover our purpose, it's essential to consider the unique gifts, talents, and abilities that God has given us. *Romans 12:6-8* says, *"We have different gifts, according to the grace given to each of us. If your gift is prophesying, then prophesy in accordance with your faith; if it is serving, then serve; if it is teaching, then teach; if it is to encourage, then give encouragement; if it is giving, then give generously; if it is to lead, do it diligently; if it is to show mercy, do it cheerfully."* God has equipped us with specific skills and passions, and by using these gifts to serve others, we can fulfill our purpose and make a meaningful impact.

Personal Reflection: Over the years, I have come to recognize the unique gifts and abilities that God has given me. By using these gifts to serve others, I have experienced a sense of purpose and fulfillment that I never thought possible.

In addition to using our gifts and talents, living a

life of purpose also involves seeking God's will for our lives. *Proverbs 3:5-6* tells us, *"Trust in the Lord with all your heart and lean not on your own understanding; in all your ways submit to him, and he will make your paths straight."* As we submit our plans and desires to God, He will guide us and lead us into the purposeful life He has designed for us.

Personal Reflection: I have found that as I trust in God and seek His guidance, He has led me into opportunities and relationships that have allowed me to make a meaningful impact in the lives of others. By following His leading, I have been able to walk in His purpose for me.

Living a life of purpose is not only about what we do; it's also about who we are becoming. As we grow in our faith and become more like Jesus, we will naturally impact the world around us. In *Matthew 5:14-16*, Jesus tells us, *"You are the light of the world. A town built on a hill cannot be hidden. Neither do people light a lamp and put it under a bowl. Instead, they put it on its stand, and it gives light to everyone in the house. In the same way, let your light shine before others, that they may see your good deeds and glorify your Father in heaven.*

10

A NEVER-ENDING STORY
Continuing Our Journey with Jesus

As we come to the end of this book, we have journeyed together through the highs and lows of living a life of faith. We have explored the importance of building a solid foundation, persevering through challenges, and growing in our spiritual disciplines. But as we conclude this book, I want to remind you that the journey with Jesus is never-ending.

In *Philippians 3:13-14*, Paul writes, *"Brothers and sisters, I do not consider myself yet to have taken hold of it. But one thing I do: Forgetting what is behind and straining toward what is ahead, I press on toward the goal to win the prize for which God has called me heavenward in Christ Jesus."* Paul recognized that his journey with Jesus was a never-ending story, with new challenges and opportunities to grow always on the horizon.

We must also remember that our journey with Jesus is not a solo endeavor. *Hebrews 12:1-2* reminds us of the great cloud of witnesses that surrounds us and encourages us in our journey. And of course, we have the Holy Spirit to guide us every step of the way.

So how do we continue our journey with Jesus? First and foremost, we must keep our eyes fixed on Him. *Hebrews 12:2* says, *"Let us fix our eyes on Jesus, the author and perfecter of our faith, who for the joy set before him endured the cross, scorning its shame, and sat down at the right hand of the throne of God."* We must never lose sight of who Jesus is and what He has done for us.

Secondly, we must stay connected to the body of Christ. In *1 Corinthians 12*, Paul describes the church as a body, with each member playing a unique and important role. We need each other to grow and thrive in our faith.

Thirdly, we must continue to grow in our spiritual disciplines. Just because we have built a strong foundation and established good habits in the past does not mean we can rest on our laurels. We must continually seek to deepen our prayer life, study of the Word, and other spiritual practices.

Finally, we must focus on the ultimate goal: eternal life with Jesus. In *Revelation 21:3-4*, John describes the New Jerusalem, the city of God, where there will be no more tears, death, or mourning. This is the ultimate destination of our journey, and we must never lose sight of it.

As we continue our journey with Jesus, we may face new challenges and struggles, but we can take comfort in that He is always with us. As Jesus said in *Matthew 28:20, "And surely I am with you always, to the very end of the age."* And with Jesus as our guide and the Holy Spirit as our helper, we can be confident that we will finish the race and receive the prize God promised us.

So let us press on toward the goal, never losing sight of Jesus and the ultimate destination of our journey. Let us stay connected to the body of Christ, continue to grow in our spiritual disciplines, and trust in the guidance of the Holy Spirit. Our journey with Jesus is a never-ending story, but with Him by our side, it is filled with purpose, hope, and joy.

11

THE AUTHOR'S RETURN
Anticipating the Second Coming of Christ

As we come to the end of this book, it's fitting to discuss the final chapter of the Christian story - the return of our Author, Jesus Christ. The Bible is clear that Jesus will come again to bring an end to this present age and establish his eternal kingdom. This event is known as the Second Coming, and it's something that every Christian should eagerly anticipate.

The Second Coming of Christ is not something to be feared or ignored, but it's a joyful and glorious event that will bring ultimate redemption and restoration. Scripture tells us that when Jesus returns, he will come with power and great glory, and all eyes will see him *(Matthew 24:30)*. He will come to judge the living and the dead, and he will separate the righteous from the unrighteous *(Matthew 25:31-46)*.

As Christians, we should long for the return of Christ, knowing that it will mean the end of sin, suffering, and death. It will also mean the beginning of a new heaven and earth, where God will dwell with his people forever *(Revelation 21:1-4)*. The apostle Peter tells us we should *"look forward to the day of God and speed its coming"* (2 Peter 3:12).

But while we eagerly anticipate the Second Coming of Christ, we must also be diligent in our lives and faith. Jesus warns us to be watchful and ready for his return because it will come at a time when we least expect it *(Matthew 24:44)*. We must not be caught off guard, but instead, we should be actively pursuing a life of holiness and obedience to God.

So, how do we prepare for the Second Coming of Christ? Firstly, we must continue to abide in Christ and seek after him daily. This means praying, reading and studying the Bible, and engaging in fellowship with other believers. We must also be actively involved in sharing the gospel with those who do not yet know Jesus so that they, too, may be saved and ready for his return.

Secondly, we must live holy and righteous lives, constantly seeking to grow in our faith and become more like Jesus. We are called to *"be holy, because [God] is holy"* (1 Peter 1:16). This means putting to death the sin in our lives and pursuing righteousness and godliness *(Colossians 3:5-17)*.

Finally, we must hold fast to our hope in Christ and

the promise of his return. The Author of Hebrews tells us to *"hold unswervingly to the hope we profess, for he who promised is faithful" (Hebrews 10:23)*. We must not be swayed by the troubles and difficulties of this life, but instead, we must keep our eyes fixed on Jesus, who is the Author and perfecter of our faith *(Hebrews 12:1-2)*.

The Second Coming of Christ is an event that we should eagerly anticipate as Christians. It's a time when Jesus will come to bring ultimate redemption and restoration to the world. But while we wait for his return, we must be diligent in our faith, pursuing holiness and sharing the gospel with others.

We must hold fast to our hope in Christ and continue to abide in him daily. And when he does return, we will rejoice and celebrate the ultimate fulfillment of God's plan for salvation. As John writes in *Revelation 22:20, "Amen. Come, Lord Jesus!"*

CONCLUSION
Embracing the Author and Finisher of Our Faith

As we end this journey, I hope you have been encouraged to embrace Jesus Christ as the Author and Finisher of your faith. He is the one who started your faith journey, and He is the one who will bring it to completion. Through the ups and downs of life, He is the anchor that holds us steady.

We have explored the various aspects of our faith journey, from its beginning to its end. We have seen the importance of repentance, baptism, and the Holy Spirit. We have learned about the challenges we will face and how we can grow through them. We have discussed the spiritual disciplines that help us build a stronger faith. We have looked forward to the promise of eternal life and the return of our Lord and Savior.

Throughout this journey, one thing has remained constant: the love of Jesus Christ for us. He loved us before we even knew Him, and He will love us for all eternity. He is the one who gave His life for us, and He is the one who will never leave us nor forsake us.

As we conclude this journey, I want to leave you with a few final thoughts:

First, embrace Jesus Christ as your Lord and Savior. If you have not already done so, make the decision to follow Him today. Repent of your sins, confess Him as your Lord, and be baptized in His name. Receive the Holy Spirit and begin the journey of faith.

Second, trust in Him through the challenges of life. Know that He is with you always, even in the darkest moments. Lean on Him and seek His guidance and comfort.

Third, practice the spiritual disciplines that help us grow in our faith. Spend time in prayer, read and study the Bible, worship with other believers, and serve others in love.

Fourth, live a life of purpose and impact. Use your gifts and talents to make a difference in the world, and share the love of Jesus Christ with those around you.

Finally, look forward to the return of our Lord and Savior. Anticipate the day when we will see Him face to face and be with Him for all eternity.

As we embrace Jesus Christ as the Author and Finisher of our faith, we can have the confidence and assurance that He will see us through to the end. He is the one who began this journey with us, and He is the one who will bring it to completion. Let us trust in Him and follow Him with all our hearts.

Hebrews 12:1-2 says, "Therefore, since we are

surrounded by such a great cloud of witnesses, let us throw off everything that hinders and the sin that so easily entangles. And let us run with perseverance the race marked out for us, fixing our eyes on Jesus, the pioneer and perfecter of faith. For the joy set before him he endured the cross, scorning its shame, and sat down at the right hand of the throne of God."

May we run the race marked out for us with perseverance, fixing our eyes on Jesus, the pioneer and perfecter of our faith. And may we one day hear Him say, *"Well done, good and faithful servant! Come and share your master's happiness!"* (Matthew 25:23)

ABOUT THE AUTHOR

Elizabeth Olufemi: A Journey of Purpose

Elizabeth Olufemi, a vibrant and inspiring individual, was born in the bustling city of Washington, D.C., with roots deeply embedded in the rich cultural heritage of Nigeria. Known for her multifaceted talents, Elizabeth is an accomplished author and a certified life purpose and goal success life coach. Adding to her diverse repertoire of skills, she holds the esteemed title of a notary public in Texas.

With an unwavering passion for healthcare, Elizabeth has dedicated many years to the industry, tirelessly working to improve the lives of others. Her commitment to making a difference extends beyond her professional endeavors, as she is also an astute entrepreneur and the proud founder of Lizzy Bee International, LLC.

Equipped with a Bachelor's degree in Health Administration, Elizabeth's pursuit of knowledge knows no bounds. Currently, she is undertaking her master's degree in Health Informatics, furthering her expertise and embracing the ever-evolving healthcare landscape.

While her professional pursuits undoubtedly shape her identity, Elizabeth's true essence shines through her love for writing. Through her words, she illuminates the human experience, uplifting and inspiring readers to discover their inner strength and purpose. Her writing reflects her deep-rooted spirituality, often drawing inspiration from spending cherished moments in God's presence.

Elizabeth's altruistic nature is reflected in her involvement in charitable works. With a heart overflowing with compassion, she endeavors to touch the lives of those in need, spreading love and light wherever she goes. Beyond her professional and personal endeavors, Elizabeth finds immense joy in her role as a loving mother—a testament to her nurturing and selfless spirit.

Now, Elizabeth Olufemi's transformative journey as an author embarks on a new chapter with her debut book. With a unique blend of wisdom, personal anecdotes, and a profound understanding of human God's way, Elizabeth invites readers to embark on a transformative journey of self-discovery and purpose. Her book promises to be a beacon of hope, guiding individuals toward unlocking their true potential and realizing their dreams.

Join Elizabeth Olufemi as she weaves together the tapestry of words, empowering readers to embrace their inherent greatness and create a life of fulfillment and joy.

Printed in the USA
CPSIA information can be obtained
at www.ICGtesting.com
LVHW071525090823
754638LV00017B/410